# GOD THINGS COME IN SMALL PACKAGES

To schedule author appearances, write: Author Appearances, Starburst Promotions, P.O. Box 4123, Lancaster, Pennsylvania 17604 or call (717) 293-0939. Website: www.starburstpublishers.com

CREDITS:
Cover design by Richmond & Williams
Text design by Steve Diggs and Friends, Nashville

All scripture was taken from the HOLY BIBLE: NEW INTERNATIONAL VERSION® NIV®. Copyright© 1973, 1978, 1984 by International Bible Society.

First Printing, May, 2000
ISBN: 1-892016-28-1
Library of Congress Catalog Number 99–69035
Printed in USA

# Contents

# INTRODUCTION

*By Susan Duke*

*There are extraordinary moments in our lives when we are certain a Divine Hand has brushed our cheek, wiped our tears, and graced our hearts with a glimpse of eternity.*—Susan Duke

*H*eavenly treasure awaits those who search for blessings that are wrapped in the smallest and most ordinary packages. Upon finding such a package, we often realize it was the package that found us!

In fact, it was God who tapped us on the shoulder and handed us a gift marked *Special Delivery*—"special" because the gift-bearer is the Almighty Creator of the universe, making himself known in the smallest most intimate ways.

How else can you explain a firefly that lights up a dark night, an unexpected airline ticket, or a single tear that opens the floodgate of healing? These are God things. The Creator loves to give gifts to his children. God things come in small packages.

It is our prayer that as you read our stories, you will be inspired to notice the special deliveries that God has sent to the threshold of *your* heart. May God's small packages bring to your life the wonder of his providence, the touch of his grace, and the fragrance of his love.

"Every good and perfect gift is from above, coming down from the Father of the heavenly lights. . . ." —James 1:17

Your heart is the wellspring of your life! Guard your heart and don't let it become hardened. Let Me strengthen your heart so that you will be blameless and holy before Me. I'll give you a new heart and put a new spirit in you. I'll replace your heart of stone with a tender heart that can love and be loved.

*Tenderly,*

*God*

———————————————————

Proverbs 4:23; Hebrews 3:8; 1 Thessalonians 3:13; Ezekiel 36:26

# HEART TO HEART

*By Susan Duke*

$\mathcal{T}$he majestic view was breathtaking—and the perfect building site for Judy and David's little mountain cabin in Arkansas. Every weekend for a year, they drove two hours from their hometown to their primitive refuge. They cleared trees by day and enjoyed cozy campfires and moonlit swims in the cool, crystalline river at night.

Through no choice of their own, a yearlong struggle with unsettling issues at their home church had left Judy and David feeling wounded and alienated even from lifelong friends. They desperately needed a haven where they could find emotional, physical, and spiritual refreshment.

Late evenings at the mountain often found Judy strolling along the tranquil, winding river, picking up rocks from the riverbank to skim across the water. One particular evening, Judy discovered she'd picked up a perfectly shaped heart rock. She didn't know why at the time, but she sensed that the unusual rock held a sort of significance. She tucked it away in her pocket and, after the weekend, took the rock home and placed it on her desk, where it sat for over a year.

One morning, while reading a devotional from Ezekiel 36:26, a sudden surge of tears began flowing down Judy's face. "A new heart will I give you and a new spirit will I put within you, and I will take away the stony heart out of your flesh and give you a heart of flesh." The words compelled Judy to go and get the heart-shaped rock from her desk.

As she clutched it in her hand, the parable of the rock was clear. It was as if God were saying, "Judy, your heart is just like this rock. Layers of unhealed hurt and attempting to shield your heart from pain have made you resist loving and allowing others to love you. Rocks don't feel and your heart has quit feeling, too. But unlike this rock, which can't be changed, I will restore a new and tender heart within you."

Today Judy tells mountain visitors who join in her rock searches along the river, "When you find a heart rock, it's God saying . . . he loves you."

God often has to do open-heart

surgery in us and replace a calloused

heart with one that trusts and risks

everything for the sweet reward of

love and life.

*I*'ve ordained all of your days.
My eyes are everywhere keeping
watch over you. Even if you walk
through the valley of the shadow
of death, you won't fear any evil
because I am with you. I save and
deliver you from all who try to
pursue you.

*My Protection,*
*Your Sovereign God*

———————— ◦ ————————

Psalm 139:16; 33:13–15; 23:4; 7:1

# PICTURE PERFECT TIMING

*By LeAnn Weiss*

$O$ ver the years, I've earned the reputation of being a shutterbug. But of the thousands of pictures I've taken, there's one in particular I'll never forget.

Driving up the mountain at the tail end of a student mission trip I was coleading in Central America, I winced when I realized I had missed a breathtaking picture. Our driver, Wayne, reassured me that a better panoramic view of the entire lake valley lay just ahead.

Thirty minutes later we stopped at the top of the mountain for my Kodak moment. Anxious for showers and shopping, the students grumbled as I snapped away. Moments after the twelve of us were back on the road, I noticed what appeared to be a police barricade in the far distance.

Looking up from gathering our passports, I exclaimed, "Hey, those police are wearing black ski masks and pointing machine guns at those people in that car!" Realizing the impending danger, I began to stuff the four thousand dollars I was carrying to pay for our trip into smelly socks.

We hadn't been spotted yet. Unable to turn around our over-loaded van on the narrow mountain road, Wayne opted to slowly reverse the van. Soon, the masked men noticed us trying to escape and hijacked another car to come after us. The bandits pulled alongside our van, screaming in Spanish as they aimed their guns. Fearing a guerrilla hostage situation, Wayne shifted the van forward and attempted to out-run them. Yelling for the teenagers to hit the floor, Wayne sped away. A spray of bullets evoked even more cries and prayers. For what seemed like an eternity, our runaway van careened down the mountainside precariously close to the cliff, as Wayne battled the wheel.

Safely reaching the foothills of the city, we were relieved nobody in our van had been shot. A bullet had ricocheted off the van, almost piercing the gas tank. All of the cars that had passed us when we stopped for my pictures had been robbed of all of their money, cameras, jewelry, and valu-ables. Every time I see the picture of our group on that mountain, I'm reminded how God's perfect timing protected us from being ambushed.

Sometimes God places unexpected

stops in our lives. Some detours yield

pleasant surprises, while others are

seemingly irritating delays. God looks

down from above, seeing the entire

picture of our lives as he orchestrates

his perfect timing knowing what is

best for us.

*N*othing in this world begins to compare to the peace I give you. Don't let your heart be troubled. No matter what obstacles you face, you don't have to fear. My law is perfect, reviving your soul. My statutes are trustworthy and simplify wisdom. Everything in My Word was written to encourage you and give you hope.

*With You Always,*
*Your God of Peace*

John 14:27; Psalm 19:7; Romans 15:4

# LOOKING FOR PEACE ON ALL THE WRONG PAGES

*By Judy Carden*

$\mathcal{I}$t is four in the morning. The house is dark, save for the soft glow from the bedrooms, where my family sleeps. But this morning I sit in solitude, all serenity eluding me.

Here in my office, I rifle through magazines. Sorting out questions. Searching for answers. And whispering wimpy prayers while I work.

Flipping through the pages, I arm myself with information on the airborne allergies from which I suffer. If educating myself on these particular medical issues is meant to ease my mind, it isn't working. And as if that isn't enough, here on my desk is the piece of paper the doctor handed to me yesterday with the diagnosis, "Squamous Cell Skin Cancer," scrawled upon it. The mere sight of the word "cancer" sends shivers up my spine.

*Prevention, Better Nutrition,* and *Runner's World* magazines are scattered about the floor near my feet. Dog-eared and high-lighted with yellow marker, the pages do little to console my health fears.

Exhausted, I head for the warmth of my bed, but stumbling through the darkness my right foot kicks something hard.

It's an old friend. One that I haven't seen for a while.

My Bible.

Tears moisten the neckband of my nightgown. Slowly, I retrieve it from the floor. It, too, is dog-eared and high-lighted. It is also dusty.

With renewed reverence I open it.

Thumbing through the pages, I am reminded how Jacob had wrestled until dawn with the angel of God near the ford of Jabbok.

With the unsettling news I received from my family doctor, I, too, am wrestling with God in my own ford of fear. So much so that I went on a personal fact-finding mission. And I didn't like the facts I found—until I read my Bible, that is.

Dawn's first light just peeked through the window. And with it, God's promise that he is with me always. At long last, calmness fills the empty crevice of my soul. I found what I'd been looking for . . . I'd simply been looking for peace on all the wrong pages.

When concerns cloud our minds and steal our serenity,

we often seek instant comfort through words of the

world. But we've been given another means, an even

better means: the complete package of God's Word.

And on those pages we will find peace beyond all earthly

understanding.

*F*aith is the substance of things hoped for. . . . Experience all of My spiritual blessings from heavenly places. I delight in doing far beyond all of your expectations and dreams according to My power which is at work in you.

*Rich Blessings,*
*Your God of Every*
*Good and Perfect Gift*

---

Hebrews 11:1; Ephesians 1:3; 3:20

# WEDDING GIFTS FROM GOD

*By Caron Loveless*

$\mathcal{L}$ike most young girls I had a dream that one day I would fall in love with a wonderful guy and while Rodgers and Hammerstein played in the background we would waltz like a prince with his princess at a fabulous fairy-tale wedding. Well, half my dream came true. I did get a prince of a guy. However, the prince I picked was a pauper and the beautiful wedding remained just a dream.

When David asked me to marry him, we were college students with barely enough money to live on, much less pay for a wedding. Adding to the financial strain was the sadness that my father, who had died several years earlier, would be missing on the most important day of my life. With no money for flowers or a dress, I told myself, "You're getting married. That should make you happy enough!" And I set my heart on a bare-bones, no-frills wedding.

Then after church one day a woman stopped me and said, "Honey, I have this great little punch recipe. Why don't you let me mix some up for your reception?" The next week someone else said, "I've had cake-decorating classes. Why don't you let me bake the cake?" Then another woman said, "Pick out whatever pattern you like and I will make your dress. It'll be my gift." The offers overwhelmed me.

Soon other women were hosting bridal showers, arranging photography, making sandwiches, and ordering flowers. And as I hugged and thanked them, each one said, "Oh, it's nothing, honey. Just see my little part as a wedding gift from God."

When the night finally came, I walked the aisle in a shimmering white satin gown toward my handsome prince. There were candles, flowers, and mountains of food, all precious tokens of God's care for me. And though my earthly father was in heaven, I knew for sure that my Heavenly Father had indeed come to earth and was present at the wedding of my dreams.

God's love for us is extravagant,

even when our faith is not. He

outdoes our expectations—he fills

the silver platter high and holds it

up for all to see his glory.

$\mathcal{B}$e careful how you live. Wisely take advantage of every opportunity that comes across your path. Stand firm in your faith during suffering. Remember that I am able to keep you from falling and to present you without fault and with great joy.

*Smile, I love you,*
*Your God of Wisdom*

Ephesians 5:15–16; 1 Peter 5:9; Jude 1:24–25

## BUBBA'S SMILE

*By Susan Duke*

If there were a poster depicting redneck dogs, Bubba would be the perfect model.

His clumsy gait and shaggy black fur only enhanced his most defining feature of all: a prominent underbite that made Bubba look as if he was wearing a perpetual smile.

When an uninvited beagle dug under the fence where Lucy, our full-blooded miniature schnauzer, romped daily, we promptly shooed him away before he became overly friendly. Unfortunately, until the surprise birth of Bubba, we had no clue our efforts had been in vain! He was a darling fur ball . . . until the puppy stage passed and Bubba's legs kept growing, along with his pointed, bushy tail. He was too rambunctious to be a house dog, but occasionally, he discreetly crawled on his belly through an opened door.

One morning as I hurriedly dressed to go speak at a ladies' luncheon, I rushed out of the bathroom into the hall. Suddenly my feet collided with what felt like a small heavy log. I fell hard against the floor, with no chance of softening the blow to my knees. Miraculously, the "small log" (alias Bubba) escaped

19

unharmed and found a hiding place. I inched my way up the wall and tried to steady myself. Pain or no pain, I had to leave.

Before my appointed time to speak, I listened to several conversations around the luncheon table. The atmosphere grew solemn, as different ladies expressed concerns over prevailing problems in their daily lives. I began rethinking my speaking topic and retreated to the ladies' room to send up a prayer flare. "Lord, touch hearts today and show me what these women need."

Without warning, searing pain shot through my swollen knee. Unkind thoughts of Bubba reigned. He was the cause of this discomfort! (*Not unlike the discomfort of some here today,* I thought.)

I never saw the sprawling trap before me because in my rush, my guard was down. (*Not unlike hearts here today*, my thoughts continued.)

If I'd known Bubba had snuck inside, I'd have watched out for him. (*There will always be unseen "Bubbas" in life*, my thoughts prevailed.)

More thoughts poured forth. I walked to the podium to deliver my newly assigned speaking topic: *Life's Bubbas*. (I could almost see the rascal smiling.)

It's the unwelcome surprises in life

that trip us up and cause us pain. But

God never misses an opportunity to

pick us up and help us learn and grow

from life's interruptions.

*I* love a cheerful giver. Give and watch Me multiply blessings back to you. Test Me! See if I will not throw open the floodgates of heaven and pour out overflowing blessings.

*Bountifully,*
*Your Awesome God*

2 Corinthians 9:7; Luke 6:38; Malachi 3:10

# THE PRICE WAS RIGHT

*By LeAnn Weiss*

$\mathcal{F}$rom the first time I spotted the soft gray L-shaped desk and hutch, I knew it would be perfect for my home office. I planned exactly where it would go. Normally, I'm a big bargain hunter, but I really wanted this desk and worked for months to save the $799 listed on the price tag. But when I learned of some desperate financial needs within my church, I felt God nudging me to help meet those needs. My dream desk would have to wait.

Almost two years later, while checking out the clearance section in that same office supplies store, I noticed a thin, three-foot-tall cardboard box with a bright red tag. When I saw that the price of $149 was marked down to $29, I couldn't help but peek inside. Figuring I could use the solid, one-inch-thick Formica cornerpiece for something, I flagged down a salesman and told him I'd take it. He seemed relieved to finally get rid of the box and told me he'd bring it up front. I was surprised when he came to the register with a loaded cart. He said the two other six-foot boxes were part of my deal.

"What's in them?" I asked curiously.

He relayed that it was supposed to be a desk, but all of the screws and hardware and some other vital pieces were missing. After paying $29 plus tax, I located a truck to haul the unexpected huge boxes home.

Not being mechanically inclined, I instead recruited my sister-in-law, Tammy, to assemble my bargain. Warning her about the missing parts, I left to run errands.

Returning home, I was shocked to see the finished product. It was my light-gray dream desk! Tammy laughed, "Didn't they read the instructions? This is one of those new prefabricated self-connecting units that doesn't use screws." Only one piece was missing and the manufacturer shipped it at no charge.

When I examined my receipt more closely, I noticed it reported that I had saved $770. I had no doubt that God had somehow marked the heavenly price tag—and the price was right.

God loves a giving heart. When we

put others' needs before our own,

he unleashes unexpected blessings

we cannot measure from his

bountiful storehouse.

$\mathcal{K}$now that I am close to the brokenhearted and save those who are crushed in spirit. No one who hopes in Me will ever be put to shame.

*Compassionately,*
*Your God of All Hope*

P.S. When you hope in Me, I'll renew your life!

———————— ⬦ ————————

Isaiah 66:13; Psalm 25:3; Isaiah 40:31

# TENDER TEARS OF HOPE

*By Judy Carden*

$\mathcal{N}$early a fortnight had gone by since the untimely passing of my thirty-three-year-old husband. The smallest survivors, our three young children, then ages three, seven, and eight, silently slipped into a canyon of despair.

I tried desperately to remain calm and strong for their sakes, but as minutes ticked into hours and hours turned into days, my own grief pulled me into the same dark canyon.

Unfortunately, we soon discovered it was business as usual for everyone else. Neighborhood children played. Teachers taught. Street cleaners swept. Restaurants fed hungry people. And at every turn, it seemed, fathers hugged their children.

One weekday afternoon, as my children were trying hard to concentrate on homework, I sensed their hearts just weren't into studying.

"Come on kids, let's take a break and go for a drive," I said as I gathered my purse and keys.

I drove to our local Wal-Mart, thinking we'd just take time to wander through the store. Silently, I prayed for a spark of normalcy, but wondered if our healing process would ever begin. Our lack of emotion frightened me. I knew we needed to cry—to express our brokenness—but tears wouldn't come. I could only pray, *God, please help us.*

A sudden clap of thunder jolted me from my thoughts.

Three-year-old Ryan whimpered, "Mommy, I'm scared."

As lightning flashed and thunder boomed louder and louder, Ryan's whimper turned to sobs. I knelt down to scoop him into my arms, hoping to calm him, but to no avail. My seven-year-old son broke next. Within moments, my valiant eight-year-old daughter and I followed suit. Like a mother hen gathering her chicks under her wing, I huddled with them on a cold floor in Wal-Mart, seeking solace in each other's embrace.

Suddenly I realized we were all crying. Tender tears finally flowed. As the thunder gave way to a gentle rain outside, I closed my eyes and thanked God for using the thunder to unite our weary hearts and release a healing stream of tears that would begin to wash our hearts with hope.

*There are times when our sadness and grief overwhelm*

*us to the point of hopelessness. But even when healing*

*seems out of reach, God is reaching out, scooping*

*us into his arms, speaking through claps of thunder,*

*"I am here."*

Y ou're a child of light. See the light shining . . . your darkness is already passing. The path of the righteous is like the first gleam of sunrise, getting brighter each moment till the full light of day. Walking in the light of My presence you'll experience blessings.

*Shine Brightly,*
*Your Father of Light*

_____    _____

Ephesians 5:8; 1 John 2:8; Proverbs 4:18; Psalm 89:15

# NIGHTLIGHT

*By Susan Duke*

$\mathcal{I}$ walked outside onto the porch, feeling as lonely and empty as the midnight sky. No stars were in sight and not even a sliver of light shone from the clandestine moon. I sat in my old rocking chair, listening for a sign of life from the bleak stillness. But the only sound that emerged from my ebony sanctuary was that of the wooden rockers that groaned beneath my weight.

I'd somehow survived several months of losses—my precious eighteen-year-old son, my best friend, a dear family friend, and a twenty-one-year-old nephew, all within a very short period of time. I had a full speaking schedule and was afraid if I rested or postponed even one appointment, I'd fall apart and never recover. I kept going physically, but like the moon, my grieving heart was hidden behind clouds of sorrow and questions.

"Lord, I can't keep going through the motions of normalcy. My life will never be the same. I can't change that—and the darkness I'm feeling in my soul is because I know you can't change what's happened either. But you must realize I can't continue this journey without your light to guide me. If I could just see a glimmer of light in all of this vast darkness, I'd believe you really do have a plan and purpose for me."

As I wept and released my grief to God, I noticed something out of the corner of my eye. Blinking ever so steadily, within the reach of my hand, was a firefly—one lone firefly that flickered and fluttered its way to my shoulder, where it landed and paused. I didn't move. Then suddenly, it darted in front of me, hovering intermittently, then swooping away and then back again, as if performing a perfectly choreographed dance of light. Luminous, dazzling, glowing light!

I beheld the gift before me—God's radiant little messenger of light that pierced the darkness and brought a message of hope.

*Even through the darkest moments of*

*our lives, God's night-light is always*

*on, ever assuring us that we are not*

*alone and that his light will guide us*

*and give us hope.*

$\mathcal{F}$rom the fullness of My grace, you have received one blessing after another. I make all grace abound to you, so you will always have everything you need to excel in every good work. Faithfully pass My contagious grace on to others. Surely My goodness and love will follow you every day of your life. You will dwell in My house forever.

*Blessings,*

*God*

—————————————

John 1:16; 2 Corinthians 9:8; 1 Peter 4:10; Psalm 23:6

# A Most Contagious Kindness

*By Caron Loveless*

*T*here's a weary old woman in the grocery line next to me and she's in a bit of a panic. I have had this panic myself a few times. To me it's the absolute worst. Your palms sweat and your cheeks go hot and folks glare like you've just botched a bank robbery.

The woman has run out of money and she's holding up the line. She's frantic and flustered and looks back and forth between the items in her cart and the money in her hand. To make matters worse . . . she doesn't speak English.

The checkout girl wants to go home and rolls her eyes at the woman. When she sees that the carts in her line have backed up to the cereal display, she lets out a sigh. Some customers are patient, but the ones buying ice cream are getting concerned.

Then a young man standing in line with the woman leans forward and tosses some cash on the conveyor belt. She gasps and waves him off but the young man says, "Hey, it's nothing, no big deal."

35

The checkout girl figures her total again, but the old woman still comes up short.

This makes another man step up and ask, "How much does she need now?"

The woman shakes her head, no, no, but you know she means, yes, yes. Her eyes get watery, so she turns her face away. She wants to thank these strangers and she tries, but what can you do when you don't speak the language? So she nods a shy thank you and picks up her groceries to leave. When she does, the men nod back to her, nonchalant, acting like they do this all the time.

What I've witnessed is a rare and selfless kindness. These men make me want to try it for myself. It's through my encounter with them that I am reminded once again of how irrational and unfathomable God's love can be. It comes when we least expect it and never leaves us stranded without hope.

God has blessed you with his kind-

ness. Why not pass it on? Kindness is

always contagious. Start an epidemic

where you live. All it takes is one to

light the way.

$\mathcal{D}$elight in My law. Character and integrity earn blessings and firmly plant you. Whatever you do, work at it with all your heart like you're doing it for Me. I'll reward your service. Be dependable where I've placed you.

*Diligently,*

*Your God of Truth*

———————————  ⬤  ———————————

Psalm 1:1–3; Colossians 3:23–24; 1 Corinthians 7:24

# ONE DEDICATED MAN

*By Judy Carden*

*O*utside the church, the long day was nearly over, and the sky bequeathed its final windblown swirls of peach, magenta, and plum. Inside, on a candlelit altar, with hundreds of eager eyes looking on, a jubilant Bob Carden pledged his love to me, and to my three small children, as well.

As the pastor spoke about the many challenges couples face in marriage, my mind wandered momentarily to matters of even greater proportion: *How would my wee ones, whom Bob soon planned to adopt, adjust to their new father? And would this marvelous man—who had prayed for a wife and children for a decade—survive?*

Three months passed. Bob's internship for instant fatherhood was intense, condensed, and hilarious. In short order, he learned the difference between thing-a-ma-jigs and whatcha-ma-callits, how to tie hair ribbons, and that not all that sloshes around in a preschooler's canteen is meant for human consumption.

Bob and the boys bonded immediately. Together, they finetuned the ancient arts of head butting, whistling, spitting, and wrestling. By all accounts, it was a match made in heaven.

Aubrey, on the other hand, hugged the sidelines. And Bob painfully recognized that her nine-year-old heart needed more time to adjust to a new daddy. "Be patient," I encouraged him. "She'll come around."

A few weeks later she did exactly that.

When a family friend ran for the Florida Senate, campaign headquarters handed out T-shirts. On the front was the candidate's name. The slogan on the back of the shirt read: "Hardworking and Dedicated . . . an Honest Man."

As Aubrey approached Bob one evening, she read the words aloud from the back of the campaign shirt he wore. "Why, Daddy," she said softly to him, "they've made a T-shirt about you."

Yes, it had taken a little longer, but heaven had finally completed the match.

The description on the T-shirt revealed to her heart what her head already knew: that God chose her second daddy especially for her, and, that he is, indeed, hardworking and dedicated . . . an honest man.

When displayed in our everyday lives, character is

obvious to those around us, making its own

declaration of love.

*T*he plans and surprises I have waiting for you are too numerous to tell! I will faithfully complete the good work I have started in you. You'll never guess all of the things I've prepared for those who love Me.

*Blessings,*
*Your God of Dreams*

———————— ⬩ ————————

Psalm 40:5; Philippians 1:6; 1 Corinthians 2:9

# ROOM WITH A HEAVENLY VIEW

*By Susan Duke*

As a new author, my first attendance at the Christian Booksellers Association was an overwhelming initiation into the publishing world. More than once, while signing books and meeting editors, I asked, "Lord, what am I doing here?"

A more than adequate, luxurious hotel suite had been pre-booked by my publisher for my four coauthors and me. And I wasn't being fussy when I wistfully voiced a childlike prayer, reminding God of my secret longing for privacy. I'd often shared a room, but on this occasion my simple heart's desire was for solitude and a temporary haven far from the noise of scheduled events.

Just as I was leaving the convention for the hotel, I bumped into the lady who'd made our reservations.

"I've been trying to find you before you left for the hotel! Unfortunately, they made a mistake in the arrangements and a couple of you are ending up with private rooms. Susan, here is the key to your room. I think you'll like it."

In the elevator, I paid no attention to the button the bellboy punched for our ascent.

Until we stepped onto the nineteenth floor. When I questioned the bellboy about why there were no doors or room numbers, he dangled the room key in the air and asked, "Don't you know where you're going, Ma'am? You're going to the Penthouse Suite—the room that presidents request when they're here!"

When he unlocked the door, I couldn't believe my eyes. The enormous four-room suite was the most exquisite I'd ever seen!

Early the next morning, as I fluffed my feathered down pillows, I sensed there was a deeper message in this divine blunder over rooms.

Gentle tears trickled down my face as I whispered, "Lord, I didn't need this room. I whined about having privacy, but a simple room would have been fine. So . . . what are you trying to tell me?"

His gentle reply came, "That I dream bigger dreams for you than you can dream for yourself."

"Indeed you do," I answered—knowing it is he who holds the key to every locked door and secret room of my heart.

*Too often we see with tunnel vision.*

*We set goals and dream dreams, but*

*fearing disappointment, dare not*

*dream too big. When God gives us a*

*glimpse of his vision for our lives,*

*the sky is the limit! He is the*

*locksmith that can open every door*

*to his dreams in our heart.*

*I*'ve given you eternal encouragement and good hope. Think about encouraging news. Reflect on things that are pure, lovely, virtuous, and praiseworthy. Cheer on and build each other up!

*Love,*

*Your God of Courage*

2 Thessalonians 2:16; Philippians 4:8;
1 Thessalonians 5:11

# THE PRECIOUS BOX

*By Caron Loveless*

$\mathcal{T}$ucked away in a drawer of my desk is a box. It's a silver-gray cardboard box that, for a brief while, lived on the shelf of a department store until I spied its sassy leather contents and carried them off to my house. Out of the box came a pair of sandals which I wore every day for an entire summer. But the seasons changed, the newness faded, and after a while I threw the sandals away. That's when I noticed the box.

The box was just wide enough and long enough to hold all the things I suddenly, for some odd reason, wanted to keep. It was the perfect weight and strength and it fit exactly where I needed it to in the bottom drawer of the desk in my room. Over time, the box served me well and it grew in such favor with me that I gave it a name: the precious box.

The precious box is like a house for my heart things. There are pictures in the pile but mostly just messages of one kind or another. Messages sent to me that, I think, one day, a long time from now, when I'm feeling lonely and unloved, I'll want to pull out and read again. Some were penned on crisp, white stationery and sent through the mail. Others were scratched on Post-it Notes and left on the kitchen counter. A few messages are from acquaintances that say how I've helped them along the way. Mostly the box holds the thoughts of people closest to me, those who've seen me at my worst and still think I'm the best.

But there's an even more important thing about this box. It seems that, when I turn my back, God gets inside.

People say you can't put God in a box. But as big as God is, he somehow manages to fit into mine. I know this is true, because months later when I open the drawer again and sort through the papers, I hear his voice on each page and feel his love in each line. Like a mystery, God sends fresh word of his care for me through all those old thank-you notes, get well cards, compliments, and kisses, reminding me that he is the giver of all good gifts.

Every good and perfect gift that comes

to you originates with God.

Sometimes his gifts come wrapped in

a human voice or message. Treasure

them all as personal presents of

encouragement.

$C$ast all your anxieties on Me, because I care for you! I am your refuge, your fortress, your God, in whom you trust. I will command My angels concerning you to guard you in all your ways. Let My peace that surpasses all understanding guard your heart and your mind.

*My Perfect Peace,*
*Your God Most High*

_____ ⚙ _____

1 Peter 5:7; Psalm 91:2, 11; Philippians 4:6–7

# A HEAVENLY RESERVATION

*By LeAnn Weiss*

*W*hen my friend Sharon's husband, Randy, told her that he had reserved tickets for their entire family to fly from Orlando to North Carolina for his grandmother's one-hundredth birthday, Sharon was petrified. She purposely hadn't flown in ten years, and he knew it.

During the next two weeks, Sharon experienced nightmares in which she envisioned dying in a plane crash. Consumed with a debilitating fear of flying, Sharon asked for family and friends to pray. Some coworkers thought it was a silly request and intensified her fear by kidding her, "Hey, you'd better pray for the pilot and other passengers, too, because it might be time for one of them to go." But several others comforted her that angels would go with her.

After an anxiety-filled flight, Sharon and her family touched down safely in Greensboro, North Carolina, and drove to High Point, where they enjoyed the celebration with family and friends.

The fun ended, and it was time to head home. As Sharon gave her name at the U.S. Air ticket counter in Greensboro to exchange her electronic itinerary for boarding passes, she was convinced that her return flight would crash. The ticket agent commented, "There are seven traveling in your party."

"No, there are only six traveling with us," Sharon corrected, naming the members of her family.

The agent turned around the computer monitor so Sharon could read the names, "Randy Myers, Sharon Myers, David Myers, Daniel Myers, Angel Myers, Laura Myers, and Emily Myers."

Before Sharon could point out the error, the ticket agent asked, "Do you have an Angel flying with you?"

Remembering that numerous friends had promised to pray, Sharon anxiously replied, "I sure hope so!"

The airline couldn't explain the mix-up. No one named Angel Myers ever showed up, but the extra ticket sparked a newfound peace during Sharon's homebound flight. Deboarding in Orlando, Sharon overheard the pilot telling the flight attendant that there had been a problem with the landing gear and some vibration. Sharon thanked God for her unseen traveling companion mysteriously ticketed on the booked flight.

God offers us his boarding pass of

peace in exchange for our excess

baggage of anxiety and fears.

*L*et Me restore your soul and guide you in paths of righteousness. I heal you when you're brokenhearted and bind up all of your hurts. I will quiet you with My love and rejoice over you. I will turn their mourning into gladness; I will replace your sorrow with comfort and joy.

*Your God of*
*Restoration*

———————  ⬦  ———————

Psalm 147:3; Psalm 23:3; Zephaniah 3:17; Jeremiah 31:13

# THE THREE BEARS

*By Susan Duke*

*B*efore twenty women arrived for an autumn day retreat, I initiated last-minute preparations: making sure the apple cider was simmering, coffeepot perking, candles lit, fire crackling, and soothing music playing.

I took a deep breath, closed my eyes, and offered a quick prayer—that all who entered our country log home would feel the warmth of God's love and presence. As soon as I said *Amen*, I had an overwhelming urge to go to the closet where I keep a stash of teddy bears, teacups, and other gift items on hand.

I followed the inner nudge to get three teddy bears and tie pink satin bows around their necks. I placed them in a sack under a cloth-covered table, just in case my nudge was God given; hidden, just in case it wasn't! Only God knew the purpose of the three bears.

The morning involved a time of casual sharing. Each lady drew a piece of paper from a basket with one word written on it, such as *peace, light,* or *joy,* and was asked to find a scripture including the word and tell what it meant to her personally.

When an older lady, Florence, read her word—*joy*—she tearfully paused before sharing why she felt her selection was no coincidence. "Joy is the one thing I've asked God to give me for over thirty years." For the very first time, Florence told her story about a sad childhood and horribly abusive first marriage.

Another lady also shared the story of her dreadfully painful childhood. By the time the last lady spoke, she revealed that she, too, had been the victim of child abuse. She had never even owned a toy.

There was a holy hush about the room.

And then . . . I knew.

I pulled the sack of bears from beneath the table and handed one to each of the three grown women who'd told their stories. Wrapped in sweet tears of joy and God's tender compassion, they clutched the bears to their hearts.

"Your Heavenly Daddy knew you'd be here today and he's instructed me to give you a teddy bear. When you look at it, remember that he is the healer of your heart and that you'll always be his little girl."

The memories we hold in our hearts are not always

pleasant. But God seeks out the brokenhearted and is

ever mindful of the healing that needs to take place in

our lives. He restores that which has been stolen and no

matter how old we get, he wants us to know we are his

precious children.

$\mathcal{J}$oy is good medicine for stress and disappointments. Don't miss out on the continual feast of a cheery heart. Remember, My joy is your strength.

*Joyfully,*
*Your God Who Heals*

P.S. Smiles bring joy.

---

Proverbs 17:22; Proverbs 15:15; Nehemiah 8:10; Proverbs 15:30

# MASHED POTATO MOUSE

*By Judy Carden*

*H*aving secured our carry-on bags in the compartment above us, Bob and I settled into seats 12 A and B on a 757 headed for Phoenix. I longed for a more intimate conversation, but after we exchanged a few formalities, an uncomfortable silence took over.

Complications stemming from his business were causing a tremendous strain in our relationship. Consequently, for the first time in our seven-year marriage, the laughter and joy that normally filled our home had all but vanished.

Once airborne, I squeezed my husband's weathered hand. Then, trading glances, my eyes held his solemn gaze. A wave of anguish swept over me, for I knew his rawboned face reflected the trepidation we both felt.

When after our first full day in Phoenix things did not improve, I resorted to the one thing I do best: I prayed.

*God*, my wounded heart whispered, *where has all the laughter gone? Be with us. Please show us how to recapture joy during times of trouble.*

The following night Bob and I joined old friends for dinner. Proceeding with caution, we listened while the others talked. Then, out of the blue, as I forked through a mound of meat and potatoes, our server tapped me on the shoulder with a most unexpected message:

"Ma'am, there's a mouse in your mashed potatoes."

Sure enough, a tiny rubber mouse had been planted in the middle of my mashed potatoes, courtesy of my friend Janan.

That was the turning point. Bob and I laughed uproariously at the mouse, and everything else that evening. And though our business problems did not magically disappear overnight, the strain in our relationship did. God saw to it that we got a heaping helping of humor when we needed it most.

To the delight of unsuspecting diners, "Mashed Potato Mouse" continues his impromptu appearances in restaurants everywhere, where the tiny, two-inch fellow is guaranteed to make you giggle. But, mostly, the mouse of the house rests at the base of the kitchen clock, reminding us that laughter, indeed, is God's sunshine for the soul.

*Laughter lightens our load,*

*especially during times of trouble.*

*It is a pep rally*

*for*

*heavy hearts.*

$C$ome to Me and you'll never go hungry. I open My hand and satisfy all of your desires, filling you with good things. Get rid of selfish ambition and vain conceit. Instead, consider others better than yourself. I'm compassionate and gracious. My anger is patient and My love abounds toward you. If you confess your sins, I'm faithful and just to forgive your sins and to purify you from all unrighteousness

*Love,*
*Your Bread of Life*

Psalm 145:16; 107:9; 103:8; Philippians 2:3;
1 John 1:9; John 6:35

# MORE THAN ENOUGH

*By Caron Loveless*

$\mathcal{M}$y husband and I are in deck chairs by the lake, watching the sun go down. We hold hands and chat and every once in a while regal swans glide by for our entertainment.

Before long a grandfather and three young children arrive. The kids notice a peanut dispenser on the dock and they yank at the grandfather's pockets for money to feed the swans.

Suddenly swans come from everywhere. You can tell they're pros at this drill. They flock toward the children like vultures, hoping we'll think they're all starving. But they don't fool us. Their bodies are round and plump.

Laughing and squealing, the kids crank out peanuts as the birds scarf their treats off the water. Most of the swans are polite, waiting their turn for more, but there is one fat, black

63

swan with horrible manners. He honks and flaps and flexes his wings and bosses the others away. The black swan is rude and the children try to avoid him, but he bullies his way to the front of the pack, paddling faster and more fiercely than the rest.

I don't like the black swan. Watching him makes me uneasy but his presence brings a lesson from God. There are times when I, too, act vulturelike, days when I'm just as selfish and tricked into fearing that others are getting ahead or gaining more than I am. Sometimes I lack the virtue and grace I was designed for. I wish it weren't true, but here in my chair on the beach I have to admit that I do wear a lot of black, and, on a few of my more ugly occasions, the swan and I could have passed for twins.

Minutes later, grandpa's money is gone; the children grow bored and run off. And as quiet returns to the lakeside I think about God's unending patience with my pettiness and thank him for this vivid reminder that when he's in charge there is more than enough for us all.

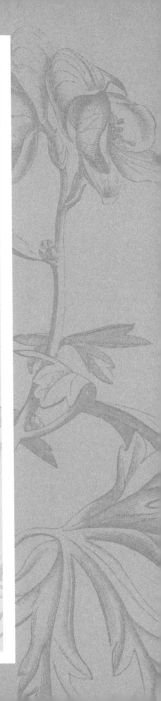

God abounds with generosity and his

goodness is poured out to all his

children. He has no favorites. And he

fills each one according to their need.

We are freed from fear and selfishness

when we learn to trust God's perfect

timing in our lives.

$W$hen you seek Me with all your heart, you'll definitely find Me! I'll instruct you and teach you in the way you should go. I'll counsel you and watch over you. Even when you grow tired and lose your way, I know the path I've custom planned for you. I encourage and strengthen you in every good deed and word.

*Guiding You,*
*Your Divine Counselor*

———————————  ———————————

Jeremiah 29:13–14; Psalm 32:8; 142:3;
2 Thessalonians 2:16–17

# CONFIRMING WORDS

*By LeAnn Weiss*

As I walked my dog Brandy late one summer night, I reviewed in my mind the unexpected phone call I had received from Washington, D.C., two days earlier, informing me that I was receiving a Presidential Appointment. Contemplating a surprise relocation, the benefits of taking the job logically outweighed any of the reasons for staying in Orlando.

But knowing God might have another plan, I earnestly prayed, "Dear God, you know I've always loved D.C., but if you want me to stay here, I'm willing. I want to be in the center of your will wherever that is."

Picking up my pace, I pictured myself in a dark wooded area. In this vision, I thought I heard God's still, small voice say, "LeAnn, over here. This is my path for you."

But when I ran to the spot where I had heard the voice in the vision, a wicked figure jumped out, taunting, "Ha! Ha!

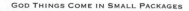

Fooled you. You missed God!" Next, I thought I heard God calling in a different direction and ran to that spot as fast as I could. This time an even larger frightening image loomed. I kept running frantically through the woods toward the voice, only to be fooled each time. My thoughts ran wild. *Does God still direct? Does God have a specific plan for my life or is following him merely a wild goose chase of hide-and-seek?* I wondered.

The next morning, I sat in our church conference room in a state of confusion, waiting for counsel from our assistant pastor. Caron Loveless, my pastor's wife, walked by and waved. A few minutes later, I felt a tap on my shoulder.

As I turned, Caron was standing there. "LeAnn, I don't know why, but I just felt impressed that God wanted me to tell you that he doesn't play hide-and-seek with you. I hope this makes sense to you because I have no idea what it means."

God accepted me where I was and used Caron's confirming words to help me find what I knew was true in my heart, reminding me of his ever present direction for my life.

Many times when we are at life's

crossroads or feel we have lost our

way, God seeks us out and sends

messengers with just the right words

to point us to his perfect custom-made

path for us.

$D$on't be weighed down by your past. See that I am doing a new thing in you. Watch life spring up! I'll bring you out of the desert and wasteland to drink of My life. Find rest in Me alone. . . . Your hope comes from Me!

*Refreshing You,*
*Your God of All Hope*

P.S. I make all things beautiful in My perfect timing.

———————— ◆ ————————

Isaiah 43:18–20; Psalm 62:5; Ecclesiastes 3:11

# FLOWERS FOR JOY

*By Susan Duke*

The gray overcast sky blended perfectly with the grayish brown pastureland that surrounded Joy's home. It wasn't exactly the kind of morning that would inspire you to go for a walk, but Joy's restless spirit pulled her outside into the cool, damp air.

Winter's bitter cold had taken a toll on Mother Nature's palette, leaving it void of color. Joy was also experiencing a winter season of emptiness, disappointment, and haunting memories of deep pain that had recently surfaced in her family. It had taken years for her to come to a place where she felt she could open the door to the past and walk back through a horrendous time in her life in order to heal emotionally. When she finally summoned the courage to open her heart, she found little consolation and understanding from those whose support she needed the most. Left feeling isolated and emotionally barren, the dreariness outside matched the sentiment in her soul.

71

As Joy walked, she prayed for answers and comfort. She ventured to the lowest point of the pastureland, where the creek spills into a small lake. Thorns pricked her jacket sleeves as she brushed past a briery thicket. When she reached the bottom of the hill, Joy spied something that didn't fit into this colorless scene. Framing the narrow creek bed was a bright yellow band. Walking closer, she saw, bursting forth from the cold, hard ground, a perfect cluster of wild yellow daisies.

She picked one of the delicate flowers and held the yellow treasure close to her face, inhaling its wild, hardy fragrance. Suddenly, it was as if new life began to bloom inside her barren heart. Growing wild, in an unlikely place, was a perfect bouquet of promise and hope.

"This is the place," she whispered, as she looked heavenward. "And this is a day of new beginnings. No longer will I let the thorns in my heart keep me bound and wounded. For I know that just beyond the thorns of pain, springs of life flow freely and there yellow daisies will forever grow."

# THE AROMA OF HIS LOVE

*By Judy Carden*

*I* had just slid into the front seat of my car, ready to drive to the ball field to watch my twelve-year-old Ryan's baseball practice. Suddenly, one of those out-of-the-blue thoughts held me back: *Stay home and bake blueberry muffins.*

I threw the thought around in my head a few times, then let it go. But as I inserted my car key in the ignition, the thought returned, this time demanding my full attention. Afraid to ignore the thought again, but feeling really silly, I climbed out of the car and headed back into the kitchen.

*Okay, so I'll bake blueberry muffins*, I conceded. And with that, I grabbed my apron and went to work.

Forty minutes passed. While I was lifting the golden brown muffins from the oven, my eldest son, sixteen-year-old Dan, plowed his way through the front foyer toward his bedroom.

"Hey Dr. D.! You're home early—how was football practice?" I inquired.

Suddenly, I heard a single thud. Sprinting through the house to his bedroom, I found him slumped on the floor, putty-gray and drenched in perspiration.

Dropping to my knees, I cradled his upper body in my arms.

"I took a helmet to the gut during practice," Dan whispered, with slow, deliberate words. "Something exploded inside," he added, pointing to his abdomen and closing his eyes.

I knew it was his spleen. Draping him over my body, I put him in my car and sped to the hospital.

After a CAT scan revealed a ruptured spleen, Dan was rushed into emergency surgery, where doctors removed his spleen.

In the wee hours of the morning, in a tiny ICU cubicle, nurses scurried, tubes dripped, and machines beeped.

"Had you not been at home, Mom," Dr. Bessler informed my husband and me when he stopped in to check on our sleeping son, "Dan would have bled to death."

To this day, whenever I detect the scent of blueberry muffins I am reminded of an awesome God and the sweet aroma of his saving love.

Obeying that inaudible voice in

our hearts sometimes seems silly.

Yet we must remember that God is

capable of extraordinary measures

in seemingly ordinary messages.

Y ou are blessed when you take refuge in Me. When you dwell in My shelter, you'll find peace from life's storms. I'll lead you beside quiet waters, restoring your soul.

*Rest in Me,*
*Your Shield and Refuge*

Psalm 2:12; 91:1–2; 23:2–3; 61:3

## STILL WATERS

*By Caron Loveless*

$\mathcal{I}$'m half awake, but my brain is already cranking through the list of people I need to see and projects that must be finished. Nothing can wait. Everything is tied to a deadline and I roll over and check the clock to see if there's time for a walk.

I really need to walk, but this is a hectic week and I waste fifteen minutes debating whether exercise is such a good idea. Then I remember I skipped two days already and that experts say it's a lost cause for women over forty who don't exercise, so I sigh and hunt for my Nikes.

Outside there's a welcome change in the weather. The air is crisp and the wind gusts hard, and I set my stride for the usual route through the golf course. It's a beautiful course with two large lakes and wide rolling hills, and I want to enjoy the view but I have chaos to sort out and worry to attend to, so that glorious green goes to waste.

The water makes an impression, though. The wind is churning every lake and pond and the dancing waves keep my interest all the way to the turnaround point.

Then across the fairway on the second hole I see something odd. The pond by the tee is smooth as glass while the wind blows all around it. It looks like a scene from *The Twilight Zone*. Then I see. On three sides of the pond stand tight clumps of trees that block out the wind. It's such a curious sight that I stop and stare, and as I do I sense a gentle message from God that says:

> *You can be as calm as this water if you stay next to me.*
> *Beyond my protection the world can be a pretty wild place.*
> *Close to me is where you'll find peace.*

I'm hungry for God's peace, so I pause to freeze the moment and for the first time notice that the pond is formed in the shape of a heart.

*God is a ready refuge for all who run*

*to him. He will shelter and shield*

*them and surround them with*

*his peace.*

$W$hat would I say? Remember, your tongue has the power of life and death. Reckless words will pierce like a sword, killing relationships. But wise words bring healing. Get rid of bitterness, anger, slander, and everything that tears down communication. Instead, choose to be kind and compassionate, forgiving others, just as I've forgiven you.

*Love,*

*Your God of Self-Control*

---

1 Peter 4:11; Proverbs 18:21; Proverbs 12:18; Ephesians 4:31–32

# GOD'S PRUNING SHEARS

*By Susan Duke*

$\mathcal{A}$s I drove up my long, winding driveway, I inhaled the scent of freshly mown grass. It was a delight to view the beautiful results of two hard days of work. Pulling weeds, planting, mulching flower beds, and trimming bushes was no easy task for me and my husband, considering the portion of acreage we had to tend.

One of my jobs was pruning the shrubs. Although I used lightweight electric shears, it was sometimes difficult to evenly clip the more delicate branches.

Gazing around the yard, I became startled when I spotted our favorite yupon holly bush. It had turned brown— overnight! This beautiful, mature plant we'd nurtured for several years looked like a withered mass of sticks. I jumped out of the car and ran to the shrub for closer observation.

It was gone, with no hope of bringing it back. My heart sank. *What could have happened?* I muttered to myself as I plopped down on the wooden sidewalk.

From somewhere deep within, I seemed to hear, *"The shrub was too severely pruned."* Suddenly, I felt sick inside. *I did this,* I thought to myself. *I wasn't careful enough. I cut too close into the fragile limbs and main arteries.*

Strangely enough, God sometimes uses stark reality to prune our hearts. As I looked at the lifeless shrub, I was reminded of sharp words that had been spoken that very week during a disagreement with a friend. We'd both said things we deeply regretted but abandoned our exposed wounds and left them to heal on their own. In the process of trying to make our points, our sharp words became instruments that severely pruned our fragile hearts and threatened to cut the life out of our relationship.

Regrettably, all I could do about the shrub was pluck it from where it had once thrived. But God showed me it wasn't too late to go to my friend and offer an ointment of love, forgiveness, and healing words that would soothe her wounded heart and help our friendship flourish once more.

Words are powerful tools that possess

the ability to wound or to heal. When

improperly used, they can cut to the

quick and bring death to something

beautiful, often without any chance of

revival. God's pruning shears trim

the debris from our hearts with close

and careful precision, helping us

mature in him.

Y ou've been saved by My gift
of unmerited favor. I've blessed
you, forgiving and covering your
sins. Approach My throne of
grace with confidence. I'll be
merciful and lavish My grace
upon you to help you in your
time of need.

*My Amazing Grace,*
*Your Mighty Savior*

———————— ❖ ————————

Ephesians 2:8–9; Psalm 32:1; Hebrews 4:16

# FENDER BENDERS
## OF GRACE

*By Judy Carden*

$\mathcal{T}$he stop sign at the corner of Main and Central was in clear view just ahead. The driver of the car in front of me saw it and stopped. The problem was, I did not—until the nose of my car met her back bumper, that is.

"Oh no," I groaned, suddenly feeling sick after hearing the *crack,* and climbed out of my shiny Sebring JXI convertible to assess the damage.

A sweet-looking white-haired lady greeted me halfway.

"Ma'am," I gushed, "please forgive me. I just took my eyes off the road for a second. Are you hurt?"

"Not a bit, dear," she answered kindly. "Are you?" she, too, inquired.

I assured her that, other than experiencing a severe case of knocking knees, I was okay. So we proceeded to inspect the cars.

"Don't worry about this old boat," said the lady, in a most gracious attempt to comfort me. "It's a 1980. Nothing could hurt it." Sure enough, she was right. For, other than a few surface scratches on its black rubber-padded chrome bumper, it was undamaged. And the same with my car—except for a few scratches and a crushed front license plate holder, all was well.

"God bless you, dear, and don't worry about a thing." And with those words, she got back into her car and drove away.

*God bless you, dear?* I replayed her words in my mind over and over again. Itwas *I* who had caused the fender bender, yet *she* was comforting *me*. She had every reason to chastise me, but instead, she forgave me. She could have bawled me out for my blunder, but instead she blessed me.

It's the same way with God, only better. For though God doesn't condone my mistakes, he doesn't condemn me either. I am forgiven because of a gift called *grace*.

Like the little white-haired lady who blessed me even though I crashed into her car, God also does the same thing—every day—when I take my eyes off the road, and especially when I least deserve it.

*God, the Prince of pardons, closes the gap between*

*failure and forgiveness for us. His great grace is our*

*salvation, and that gift takes the guesswork out*

*of the "fender benders" of life.*

*I*'m near when you call upon Me. I hear your cry and save you. I've redeemed you and called you by name. You are Mine! When you feel like you're drowning in life's circumstances, I won't let you be overwhelmed. And I won't let the fires of life burn you. Your flesh and your heart might fail, but I am the strength of your heart and your portion forever.

*Comforting You,*
*Your Living God*

Psalm 145:18–19; Isaiah 43:1; Psalm 73:26

# THE ROSE

*By Caron Loveless*

The pregnancy comes as a not-so-welcome surprise. It's bad timing. We're busier than ever. Our boys left preschool long ago and we've gotten attached to sleeping through the night. The adjustment will be tough, but we decide to look for the positives in a seemingly negative development.

We say a baby keeps you young, makes you roll on the carpet and act spontaneous. We warm to the thought of raising another heir. But what if it's a girl? Pink. How would we handle pink? Suddenly pink is everywhere. So are babies in strollers and women with basketball stomachs.

Days later we're sold on the idea. We tease and laugh about it. We talk of nurseries, test out names. I think Rose is a nice middle name. For a while we'll keep our little secret. I really want this child.

But I can't have it.

I start to bleed.

Some women have spotting and their babies make it just fine, but not me. When the cramps get bad I go to bed and when it's all over I cry myself to sleep.

In the morning I drag myself to the window and look out with sad, swollen eyes. On the porch there's a pot with a rosebush in it. The bush hasn't bloomed in months. But today something's different. During the night the bottom branch has given birth to a perfect white rosebud. And suddenly I know where it came from. I hadn't needed it yesterday. Tomorrow would be too late. Staring at it through the glass I feel touched in a very deep place. Tears slip out of the corners of my eyes. I think that if the rose could talk, this is what it would say:

*God sent me.*
*I am a memorial for this moment.*
*He sees your broken heart. He knows about the child.*
*He knows.*

So I go to the kitchen and rifle through a drawer until I find a pair of scissors. Then I walk outside, snip the rose, and kiss it.

God is near those crushed in spirit.

He sees every tear, feels every pain.

When no one else can possibly

understand the condition of your

soul, God knows. If all you can do is

breathe, he is as close as

that breath. Collapse

in his outstretched arms.

*B*ecause of My extravagant love for you, I made you alive with Christ, even when you were hopeless. In My great mercy, I've given you a new birth into living hope through Jesus' resurrection power. You are being transformed into My likeness with an ever increasing glory, which comes from Me.

*Always,*
*Your God of Love*

———————————— ⬤ ————————————

Ephesians 2:4–5; 1 Peter 1:3; 2 Corinthians 3:18

# A VERY SPECIAL GIFT

*By LeAnn Weiss*

$\mathcal{W}$ith Easter approaching, Lynda was reading a devotional about the Lord's Crucifixion during her morning quiet time. As she read and sang, the Easter story seemed to come alive. Touched by the pain and suffering Jesus must have experienced as he hung on the Cross for her sins, Lynda cried, thanking God for his love gift at Calvary. It was one of those special worship encounters she knew she'd always cherish.

As Lynda drove to work at Castle's Christian Book Center, she bubbled with an attitude of gratitude toward God. After their staff prayer meeting, she opened the bookstore and found that Robert and his wife were waiting at the door for her with big smiles. "As I was praying for you this morning, I felt that God wanted me to bring you this gift," he said as he handed Lynda the crude homemade plaque.

In the center of the rough piece of split bark, two twigs had been tied together to form a cross. A crown of thorns was attached to the top of the cross. Painted red nails signified Jesus' nail-pierced hands and feet and a purple ribbon symbolized royalty. Tears came to Lynda's eyes as she remembered reflecting on the Cross earlier that morning.

The gift was especially significant coming from Robert. Before he became a Christian, Robert had been a member of an east L.A. gang and his six-year heroin addiction had destroyed many people's lives. Aware of the damage he had done to his own family, a remorseful Robert had begged God for a second chance. Now, five years after committing his life to God, Robert stood as a changed man, visibly demonstrating the transforming power of the Cross.

At home later that evening, Lynda attached a note to the back of the plaque saying, "Wow, a present from God, April 1999." She lovingly hung the plaque on her kitchen wall, realizing that Robert was merely the messenger. Each time she sees the plaque, Lynda is reminded that God loved her so much that he sacrificed his only Son. Her heaven-sent plaque is a tangible memorial of his love for her.

*God doesn't love you for what you've*

*done or who you are. He loves you*

*because he is the Father of love. And*

*nothing can separate you from his*

*unfailing love.*

$\mathcal{T}$he world places a value on outward appearances. But My prime concern is the heart. Earthly things don't last, but I'm renewing you from the inside out—day by day. You are being transformed into My likeness with an ever increasing glory.

*Gloriously,*
*Your King of Kings*

———————— ⬤ ————————

1 Samuel 16:7; 2 Corinthians 4:16; 2 Corinthians 3:18

# THE TARNISHED TRAY

*By Susan Duke*

Just as Robin and her son were leaving her in-laws' house, her father-in-law, who has Alzheimer's disease, looked at Robin and said, "Wait, Robin, I have something for you."

He left to get something out of a storage building behind his house. When he returned, his eyes were shining. "Robin, this is for you. I know you'll take good care of it."

Robin's mother-in-law touched her arm and whispered apologetically, "You don't have to take that old ugly tray, dear. He's just not thinking clearly."

"Oh, that's okay. I'll take it and see if I can clean it up," Robin graciously replied.

Robin took the large, round tray home and left it on her porch for more than a week before taking it out to her husband's workshop. "I wonder what's under all this corroded black gunk? Do you have anything we can use to clean a spot on this tray and see what it's made of?"

Wesley found a tiny bit of tarnish remover and a scrap of cloth, and began polishing a small area of tray. To Robin's delight, the spot revealed that beneath the ugly, greenish brown tarnished layers was a foundation of shining, bright brass. She knew, however, that it would take many patient hours of work to make the tray beautiful.

Robin had been attending a Bible study and sincerely asking God to give her a heart after his own. During a prayer one day, she had a mental picture of the old tarnished tray with its one shiny spot. God revealed to her that, like the old tray, cleaning her heart would also take a lot of hard work. There was a shiny spot that shone brightly for him, but Robin saw that there were still a lot of grime and dark places of selfishness and greed in her heart that needed cleaning up.

The tarnished tray has become a work in progress for Robin. Each time she polishes another area, she prays that God will continue the same work in her heart—cleaning and polishing until he can see nothing but a reflection of himself.

What does God see when he looks in

your heart? When we allow him to

polish out the dark places, we are

allowing him to make our hearts

something beautiful and bright so that

we might shine and

reflect his glory.

$\mathcal{M}$ay you catch a glimpse of My outrageous love for you! Don't forget all of My benefits. I forgive your sins and heal your sicknesses and redeem your life from the pit. I crown you with love and compassion. I have called you and I won't ever let you down.

*My Forever Love,*
*Your Faithful God*

———————————  ⊙  ———————————

Ephesians 3:17–19; Psalm 103:2–4;
1 Thessalonians 5:24

# FOREVER, REGARDLESS

*By Caron Loveless*

The biggest, most beautiful hibiscus bush in the neighborhood sits in my front yard. It's about eight feet wide and ten feet tall, and fifty to sixty bright red flowers hang out from its branches every day, rain or shine, despite the fact that I have completely ignored it for the whole two years we've lived in this house.

Oh, we've trimmed the bush once or twice so we could back the car out of the driveway without getting scraped, but I've never fertilized it, or sprayed it for bugs, or paid it much notice. I've just been too busy to care.

Not long ago I was getting out of my car when I sensed God saying, "*Look at the bush.*" It reminded me of the time he spoke to Moses. Naturally, there are a couple of differences between Moses' bush and mine. Moses' bush was on fire and the word God had for me wasn't audible. I just felt him trying to get my attention. And what I heard him say was this:

103

"*Many times you have forgotten me but I am perennially and perpetually here, stationed on call in your life. I am faithful, dependable, and steadfast even when you go about your business living like you don't even know my name. No matter what you do, I am always with you. My heart toward you stays constant regardless of your love for me. I am not like others who require your love like a ransom. I will be here for you . . . forever.*"

God's love remains in constant bloom no matter how hot

or cold our affection runs toward him. Though he longs

for a relationship with us, he does not demand it.

He waits patiently, offering his best, most beautiful

gifts with no strings attached.

*B*e still and know that I am God! In your day of trouble, I'll answer when you call. No one compares to My reliability and deeds. I've been given a Name above all names. One day every knee will bow and every tongue will confess that I am Lord.

*Majestically,*

*Jesus*

---

Psalm 46:10, 86:7–8; Philippians 2:10–11

# THERE IS A NAME

*By Judy Carden*

"I'm going to get the kids," I yelled to my husband. On my way out of the house I paused to snatch some candy corn from the Halloween dish on the dining room table. Then off I drove to their elementary school.

While tuning the radio in the van, something struck me funny and I drew in my breath to laugh, inhaling the candy corn I had been sucking on. The digital clock read 2:31 P.M.

A minute passed. Then two. I commanded myself to continue driving, for common sense dictated that I was in dire need of assistance from someone other than myself.

Two more minutes passed. Barely able to drive, I braved a glance in the mirror.

My lips were blue! It was at that moment that I envisioned the newspaper headlines for the following day: WINTER HAVEN WOMAN DEAD FROM CHOKING INCIDENT

*Oh, God!*, my mind screamed. *Please, don't let me die! Not now. Not like this.* But the candy remained lodged in my windpipe.

Miraculously, I approached the rear entrance of the school. The clock read 2:36. Though my vision was beginning to blur, I spotted a van in the distance. I recognized the vehicle as belonging to my friend, Gerri, for on the lower left front corner was her trademark license plate—one bearing the name *Jesus.*

My eyes transfixed on that precious name, Jesus. I knew he was going to answer my cries of help through Gerri. So, with my last ounce of strength, I jammed the gearshift into park, opened the door, and tumbled to the ground.

Seeing this, Gerri sprang into action. Praying for guidance, she lifted my limp body from the dirt driveway and performed the Heimlich maneuver on me, clearing my airway on her third attempt.

In a moment of life or death, I called upon the Name of names. One look was all it took—seeing the name of Jesus, so small but so mighty. I will never forget that he's only a whisper away . . . and his name is life.

Jesus. A name so simple, yet so

sovereign. The name that causes

eyes to mist, knees to bend, and

choirs of angels to sing. And he's

only a prayer away.

*E*ven before you ask, I know just what you need. Come to Me for refreshment when you are worn out and worried. When you wait upon Me, I'll renew your strength. You'll rise up with wings like eagles. You'll run through life's ups and downs without growing weary and you'll walk through trials without quitting.

*Taking Care of You,*
*Your Provider and*
*Great Physician*

———————  ⊙  ———————

Matthew 11:28; Matthew 6:8; Isaiah 40:31

# PAID IN FULL

*by LeAnn Weiss*

𝒜s I sat in the waiting room for several hours, I felt drained physically, emotionally, and spiritually. I'm rarely sick and have only been to a doctor a handful of times. People frequently compare me to the Energizer bunny but my home-based business was struggling financially and I was holding a second job to make ends meet, growing more weary and rundown by the day.

After my sister and several friends feared my monthlong cold and deep croupy cough had developed into walking pneumonia or mono, they finally insisted that I see a doctor immediately. Discovering that my family doctor had closed his practice several years earlier, I called my church and was referred to Rica, one of our members. I hadn't considered Rica because I thought she was a pediatrician.

While waiting for my appointment, I wondered, *How am I going to pay for this?* I'd tried cutting expenses, and only carried catastrophic health insurance with a high deductible, and my credit cards were near their limits.

I was the last patient of the day. "Hi, LeAnn. Sorry you had to wait so long. I don't even have to ask how you're doing . . . I could hear your pathetic cough all the way down the hall . . . you poor thing," Rica said entering the examining room.

As Rica examined me, she mentioned how some of the personalized magnets, bookmarks, and other little things I had done for her and some of the other single moms at my church had ministered to her.

"It's a good thing that you came in today. You have severe bronchitis with patches of pneumonia," she said before leaving to write my prescriptions. I'd handed Rica my credit card but when she returned with a bag full of several hundred dollars worth of antibiotics, she handed me my card and said, "God wants you to know that he hasn't forgotten about you and has many other blessings awaiting you."

She placed the bill in my hand and said, "This is a love gift from God." The bill was stamped "$0.00—PAID IN FULL."

God knows each of us personally and

individually.  When we become weary

in well doing, he reminds us that there

is rest and refuge in him. The Great

Physician is always on call, eager

to tend our ailing

circumstances, and his services are

free of charge.

$\mathcal{D}$on't worry about tomorrow.
My eyes are on you. I'm attentive
to your prayers and will provide
all of your needs according to My
endless riches in glory. Put your
hope in My unfailing love.

*Love,*

*Your 100% Faithful*

*Father*

————————————  •  ————————————

Matthew 6:25; 1 Peter 3:12; Philippians 4:19;
Psalm 33:18

# THE ENVELOPE

*By Caron Loveless*

$\mathcal{W}$e're used to doing without. Money is always scarce, but this time we're really desperate. There's no gas in the car, the rent is past due, and all we have left to eat is a bag of oranges.

That's why my husband is up early, praying.

David is a graduate student and works two jobs so I can stay home with the baby, and one day a week he meets with another student for spiritual mentoring. They're both studying theology and the thing they're most passionate about is making a difference with their lives. Some mornings they are so dedicated and full of faith that they meet at five o'clock to pray in our living room.

This morning their praying is urgent.

The men take turns praying out loud. David admits he is worried but believes God can do the impossible, and he repeats this over and over in his prayer. The other man agrees and pleads for God to do something soon for his friend.

In a short while they finish praying and look up to see a small white envelope on the floor. It wasn't there before and David bends down to pick it up. When he opens it, he is speechless. Inside the envelope is seventy-five dollars in cash. There is no note or clue as to how it got there. For a moment they try to speculate. Could someone have slid it under the door? No, the threshold is too tight. And if the door had opened wouldn't they have noticed a draft? Maybe someone tucked the envelope in David's Bible and this was the moment God chose for him to discover it. They might never know.

However it arrived, the men sense that they've witnessed a miracle and they feel like shouting, but that would wake the baby. So they stifle their joy with hugs and grins and marvel together at the wonder of God.

When I wake up David beams as he puts the miracle in my hand. I am awestruck and ecstatic. It is more money than I have held in a long time, but in this astounding moment in our lives it's my faith that receives the greatest gain.

*God's ears are open to the desperate in*

*heart. His eyes are aware of their*

*need. Ask him to visit your most*

*hopeless situation. God is always*

*looking for a place to put a miracle.*

$\mathcal{I}$ know the plans I have for you. You can strategize and map out your life. . . . But I'm the one who ultimately determines your steps. If you rise on the wings of the dawn, or even if you settle on the far shores. . . . Wherever you go, My Sovereign hand will be guiding you forever.

*My Divine Guidance,*
*The Pilot of Your Life*

————————— ⊙ —————————

Jeremiah 28:11; Proverbs 16:9; Psalm 139:9–10

## MASTER OF THE WIND

*By Judy Carden*

On April 5, 1997, when dawn's first winds lifted the hot air balloon carrying Lakeland, Florida, attorney Kingswood Sprott, Jr., and his son Woody, my husband's business partner, from the north shore of Lake Wailes, they assumed the winds, as always, would be their guide. Little did they know, the very winds that lifted them would, in fact, land them in a location that they could not, in their wildest dreams, have imagined.

After enjoying a successful flight, world-class balloonist Kingswood searched for more than ten minutes for a place to land. He finally attempted a landing on the shores of Lake Ruby, ten miles due northwest, in the city of Winter Haven. But, to his chagrin, the wind sent them a little farther—crashing into the backyard fence surrounding the home that Teri and Gary Baucum had purchased just three weeks earlier.

As the Baucums approached the balloon, checking to see if the men were hurt, Kingswood introduced himself.

Upon hearing his name, Teri Baucum's spine tingled, knowing their crash landing was no accident at all. "I have your ring," was all Teri could bring herself to say.

Kingswood was mystified, for he had never so much as even met this woman.

While the three men assessed the damage to the balloon and fence, Teri returned to the house and retrieved the ring from a bureau drawer.

The ring, it turns out, was Kingswood's 1956 college ring from Washington and Lee University in Lexington, Virginia, and it had been lost for over thirty years.

In June of 1978, Teri Baucum had been swimming in Lake Wailes, the same site as the balloon launch, when she found a ring with "K Sprott Jr." inscribed on it. After several attempts to find the owner, however, Teri tucked the tarnished ring away in a jewelry box, believing it would take an act of God to locate him.

She never dreamed that God, the *Master of the Wind,* would do just that—drop K. Sprott Jr. into her own backyard, reuniting him with the ring she had found nineteen years before.

God, our Master Pilot, always plots a perfect course for

his beloved passengers, never leaving any of life's

landings to randomness.

## OTHER BOOKS BY
## STARBURST PUBLISHERS®

*God Things Come in Small Packages for Moms: Rejoicing in the Simple Pleasures of Motherhood*
*Susan Duke, LeAnn Weiss, Caron Loveless, and Judith Carden*
From life as a soccer mom to the first grandchild, most mothers spend their days taking care of others. Now, busy moms will be reminded that God is taking care of them through poignant stories recounting the everyday blessings of being a mother. Each story combines personalized scripture with heartwarming vignettes and inspiring reflections
(cloth) ISBN 189201629X **$12.95**

*God Things Come in Small Packages: Celebrating the Little Things in Life*
*Susan Duke, LeAnn Weiss, Caron Loveless, and Judith Carden*
God's generosity is limitless and His love can be revealed in many forms. From a single bloom in winter to a chance meeting on a busy street, readers will be encouraged to acknowledge God's generous hand in everyday life. Personalized scripture is artfully combined with compelling stories and reflections.
(cloth) ISBN 1892016281 **$12.95**

*God's Abundance for Women: Devotions for a More Meaningful Life*
*Compiled by Kathy Collard Miller*
Following the success of *God's Abundance*, this book will touch women of all ages as they seek a more meaningful life. Essays from our most beloved Christian authors exemplify how to gain the abundant life that Jesus promised through trusting Him to fulfill our every need. Each story is enhanced with Scripture, quotes, and practical tips providing brief, yet deeply spiritual reading.
(cloth)    ISBN    1892016141 **$19.95**

*Treasures of a Woman's Heart: A Daybook of Stories and Inspiration*
*Compiled by Lynn D. Morrissey*
Join the best-selling editor of *Seasons of a Woman's Heart* in this touching sequel
where she unlocks the treasures of women and glorifies God with scripture,
reflection, and a compilation of stories. Explore heartfelt living with vignettes
by Kay Arthur, Emilie Barnes, Claire Cloninger, and more
(cloth) 1-892016-25-7 **$18.95**

Purchasing Information
www.starburstpublishers.com

Books are available from your favorite bookstore, either from current stock or
special order: use title, author, and ISBN. If unable to purchase from a bookstore, you may order direct from STARBURST PUBLISHERS. When ordering
please enclose full payment plus shipping and handling as follows:

Post Office (4th class)
$3.00 with purchase of up to $20.00
$4.00 ($20.01–$50.00)
8% of purc hase price for purchases of $50.01 and up

Canada
$5.00 (up to $35.00)
15% ($35.01 and up)

United Parcel Service (UPS)
$4.50 (up to $20.00)
$6.00 ($20.01–$50.00)
12% ($50.01 and up)

Overseas
$5.00 (up to $25.00)
20% ($25.01 and up)

Payment in U.S. funds only. Please allow two to three weeks minimum (longer overseas) for
delivery. Make checks payable to and mail to: Starburst Publishers®, P.O. Box 4123,
Lancaster, PA 17604. Credit card orders may be placed by calling 1-800-441-1456, Mon–Fri,
8:30 A.M. to 5:30 P.M. Eastern Standard Time. Prices are subject to change without notice.
Catalogs are available for a 9 x 12 self-addressed envelope with four first-class stamps.